OLIVE JUICE FOREVER

OLIVE JUICE
FOREVER

Confessions of a Love Junkie

LORRAINE & SHAWN JENSEN

ILY PUBLISHING COMPANY
NANAIMO, BC

DISCLAIMER
The advice contained in this material might not be suitable for everyone. The authors designed the information to present their opinion about the subject matter. The reader must carefully investigate all aspects of any decisions made before committing him or herself. The authors obtained the information contained herein from sources they believe to be reliable and from their own personal experiences, but they neither imply nor intend any guarantee of accuracy. The authors are not in the business of giving legal, financial or any other type of professional advice. Should the reader need such advice, s/he must seek services from a competent professional. The authors particularly disclaim any liability, loss or risk taken by individuals who directly or indirectly act on the information contained herein. The authors believe the advice presented here is sound, but readers cannot hold them responsible for either the actions they take or the result of those actions.

Library and Archives Canada Cataloguing in Publication
Jensen, Lorraine, 1961–
Olive Juice Forever: Confessions of a Love Junkie / by Lorraine & Shawn Jensen.
– 1st ed.
1. Love. I. Jensen, Shawn, 1966- II. Title.
BF575.L8J46 2006   158.2   C2006-904412-0

ISBN 0-9781183-0-8

Cover and character design by:
Richard Hatter, Impact Visual Communications Ltd.
Cover photo: Malcolm Johnson
Senior editor and GMU: our Debbie (Schug)

ILY Publishing Company
3464 Blackfoot Way
Nanaimo, British Columbia
V9T 6M5

Printed & Bound in Canada

This book is lovingly dedicated to

ANNIE POTTINGER

love *is* the answer

And now we get to say thank you...

You know who you are, the people who love and support us and laugh at our jokes. You've held our hands and held our hearts, and some of you have kicked our butts. You've read our book, watched our children and held our vision.

Thank you to every artist who sings or writes or paints about love, and to everyone who breathes more love into this world.

To the people we have hurt we say sorry, and to those who have hurt us we say thank you. Without experiencing the pain that we have given and taken, we wouldn't be so passionate about supporting others to find their way to love.

Olive Juice Forever

Lorraine & Shawn

Foreword

The intention of this book is great enough to create a wave of love in the universe. I am so proud of my mum. She has fought to be right about love, and now she is sharing her battles and successes with the world. Love is a choice, and over the years I have watched her fight against love like a warrior. She has had to consciously turn her battles around to embrace love.

"When you change your mind, you change your life." Living in our home, you may hear that once in a while. It's true, and it has worked for us. My parents have a beautiful relationship that embraces me, my daughter and my new brother and sister. I am truly grateful. They are being what they want us to be. They honestly do walk the talk.

Watching this book go from a dream into reality has been an amazing process. The pages have already been cried, laughed and prayed over. My parents have practiced support and patience together, but most of all they have had a vision and stayed focused on it. This book is an act of love they created together, and I am so very proud of both of them.

Love & Blessings

Andrea *(a.k.a. Pumpkin)*

Table of Contents

Learn from yesterday, live for today, dream of tomorrow

Preface

A word from Shawn...

I'm just a guy. I like to hang out and have a few drinks, watch the game, get a little exercise, and listen to music.

I'm married to an ultra-intuitive, relationship-guiding, self development guru. When we got together, I was afraid of all the stuff she knew, the way she talked and the way she saw through others.

As different as we are, we are also so much alike: we love love.

We have both been through the relationship wringer and didn't want to end up there again, caught in the cycle of mistrust, fear, low self esteem, insecurity, of not showing up as who we really are. We've been there and we didn't like it.

What we do like is each other. We have both brought the bad and the good with us into this relationship, laid it out on the table, taken the best of it, and we're working at leaving the crap behind. We've set some goals and put some strategies in place to support our relationship through the tough times and through our successes. Great things have started to happen. Together we are focused on what we want and we're moving closer to our goals and dreams.

What we found is that other couples are interested in what we're doing and want to learn how to keep their own love alive. So we created our company, Olive Juice Forever, and wrote this book.

In this book we share the stories and the struggles, the tears and the fears and the games we play. We offer the tools and experiences we have both learned from in our lives, and the commitment we have made to use them.

Our life is in no way perfect. When things go sideways on us, we don't run away, we stand and face our fears. We don't shut down, we speak the truth, we course correct and we get on with it.

At times in this book I get to say my piece, to tell a bit of my story.

I'm just a guy.

Shawn

Introduction

If you are wondering where the title of this book came from I'll tell you. When you mouth the words "olive juice" it looks like "I love you." If you want to know where the rest of the title, Confessions of a Love Junkie, came from, just read the book.

I have always known *love is the answer*, it's the way I have searched for the question that has gotten me into trouble.

I used to be ashamed of my relationship history and would try and cover up the relationships I have had or the fact that I had been married twice before I married Shawn. Now I celebrate. What I know about myself is that I don't give up. Who better to stand in front of people and talk about the hardships and joys of creating an open, healthy and loving relationship than someone who has fallen flat on her face more than a few times, and keeps getting up to dust herself off and carry on. That would be me.

This book is written in three parts: yesterday, today and tomorrow. How we got to be where we are, where we are and where we are going. This book offers tools and insights into why we do some of the things we do, solutions to change if you want, and the comfort that we are not alone.

We suggest that you read this book once, then go back and review each chapter one at a time, taking the time to work on each action step. You can also go straight to any chapter to address a particular issue currently challenging you in your relationship. Each chapter also ends with an action step and has a downloadable worksheet located on our website at: www. OliveJuiceForever.com

All you need on this journey is an open and willing heart. However you use this book, know that Shawn and I are with you.

I love my life.

Lorraine

PART ONE

YESTERDAY

CHAPTER ONE

Baggage

Baggage... I'm not talking about the suitcases you take on vacation, but the crap you drag around from relationship to relationship. The "stuff" you hang onto from the past because you think it will keep you safe, but it only keeps you suffocated and scared to give love a chance. I'm talking about the chains that bind you and smother your heart, your hips and your lips.

Have you ever seen someone at the airport with really nice matching luggage? And then they get pulled aside at customs, and you get to see that all their belongings are just shoved into that fancy little bag? Pushed in there really tightly? Those bags look really good on the outside, but when you get a peek at what's on the inside, you can see that some of that laundry hasn't been aired in a while.

Have you ever noticed that in a new relationship, when the shit starts to hit the fan, it's the same issues as in the last relationship and the one before that? Have you chosen partners based on the fact that they are the total opposite of the last one, and then when trouble erupts it's the same issues again, they just look a little different?

Have you ever said, "Once bitten, twice shy?"

Just because my cat Twinkle ran away when I was four doesn't mean every cat I ever have will run away.

Just because my ex slept with someone else for six months and didn't have the guts to tell me, doesn't mean everyone else will cheat and lie.

So why do I continue to act as if they will?

My friend Judy is in a relationship with a really nice guy. Every time I ask her what it is that she loves about this guy, her answer is always the same: he's safe. Her ex husband had an affair. Say no more. Judy's afraid, and protecting herself from getting hurt again in the same way. The baggage she brings into the new relationship is the fear of abandonment, of rejection or of looking stupid. She is so scared that the new guy will do the same as her ex husband that she isn't giving him a chance to show up as himself or to be more to her than just "safe." What if he were to come home at the end of the day with tickets to Vegas or something spontaneous? How would she react? Probably thrilled and afraid at the same time. The fear would probably show up first because his actions would be so out of the ordinary that she would panic as she feels "unsafe."

As much as I love my life and my husband, we both have baggage that we brought into this relationship and we have had to work to build trust between us. It isn't that we don't trust each other; it's that we have been hurt and we each have to earn the right to one another's trust.

I came home one night eager to see my man but I couldn't find him. I started getting excited because sometimes he'll be waiting for me in the tub or somewhere I wouldn't be expecting him. I certainly didn't expect to find him in the garage sweeping the bristles

7

right off the broom. When he wouldn't look at me and just said hello while continuing to brush the cement off the floor, I gathered this as evidence that something was wrong. As it happens something was wrong: I had left my old hotmail account open and he had decided to go looking for evidence of his own. Evidence that would prove that I didn't love him, that he wasn't special and that just like the rest of the men in my life, he would end up on some heap of Lorraine's discarded men.

Well, he found it. He asked me to come into the office and showed me one of the emails he had found from my ex. I sat stunned and didn't know what to do. My stomach was in knots and I just wanted to cry. I sat in a chair by the window and told him how sad I was that he had done that. I was sad that he had found the email, because I know how horrible it feels to look at someone's personal letters and have to own up to it (or not), and to carry around in my head the stuff I have seen. I was saddest about the fact that he had to go and look for evidence of negative things when there is so much evidence for the positive around our home and in our lives every day.

8

Shawn's story:

A good friend of mine said, "What the @#%* were you thinking, looking at that email?"

Well, you know what? I've attracted and created mistrust in my life and why on earth would this relationship be any different? I was determined not to end up on Lorraine's discarded men pile. I needed to protect myself by proving that she, like the others, couldn't be trusted.

After reading that email between Lorraine and her former partner, I made up a story that I would end up just like the rest of the men in her life: dumped. I had no real proof of this, and that email was really old. However, after reading it, my thinking got away on me and my reaction to what I had been reading was as irrational as reading the email in the first place. My fear became all consuming.

If you have ever looked through someone's personal belongings, or have read their email searching for proof that your partner isn't as trustworthy as they claim to be, you know how sickening and gut wrenching this can be.

For me, trusting isn't easy to do sometimes, but now, each time I go to that place of fear or mistrust, I just say to myself, "I'm done searching for this caustic evidence and I'm done feeling this way."

I'm not proud of my actions, and it did help me to realize that I had to stop looking for the negative evidence

9

that doesn't exist in this relationship and learn to just say, "I'm done." I'm done waiting for the hammer to fall, and I'm ready to get on with it.

What an absolute waste of time and energy that experience was, time and energy that could've been spent being happy and grateful for what Lorraine and I do have.

Shawn

That night we talked about Shawn's hurt hunt. Just like me and the rest of the world, Shawn had been hurt in the past and didn't ever want to have that experience again, he wants to protect himself from that pain. And as much as he wants to protect himself from being hurt again, he also wants a loving, deep and spiritual relationship. The sad thing is that he really doesn't stand a chance at an intimate relationship when he is so afraid to open up and be vulnerable. He told me at one point that he just wants to be safe. Well, how can you be safe and vulnerable at the same time? If I'm playing it safe, I will always protect myself from hurt.

Vulnerability is almost the opposite of that: allowing myself to be exposed to potential pain. It means putting down my shield and letting my partner see who I am, trusting that he will still love me even though I'm not always the warrior woman that I project.

Can we trust ourselves to honour our feelings and say it anyway, to stand in the face of fear and express our emotions, whatever they are? If we don't, we are forever protecting ourselves from past hurts. Past hurts that may never happen again. If we live our lives in fear of re-experiencing the past, nothing will ever change.

It's my subconscious that keeps me looking for evidence. My subconscious is home to every experience I have ever had. My subconscious coupled with my ego is my greatest protector. As a team, they go to great lengths to protect me from any kind of hurt or embarrassment, and I am very grateful for that. But this also keeps me stuck in my past, afraid of doing anything that might cause pain, like taking a risk or living to my full potential.

My subconscious persuades me that "it's not worth it," or "he's just like the rest of them and will screw you over." Well, guess what? When I really want to be right about everyone being out to hurt me, I will find evidence to support my fears.

I was having coffee with a friend who was telling me about a new woman who he is crazy about. But he doesn't want to rush into another relationship since his marriage only recently ended. His reason for not getting into a new relationship: he doesn't want to drag his old baggage along with him. He's worried that his wife left him because he didn't have enough energy and passion for life, and he doesn't want to be that way with this new woman. I asked him what he thought he was going to do with his past, leave it on the doorstep when he goes into the new woman's house?

I don't care why you stay out of relationship, unless you work on yourself, you'll still have the same old reactions in the next relationship. In a new relationship, everything is all exciting and fresh, but I am still bringing along me — the exact same me — that was in the last relationship and the one before that.

It's easy for me to be single. I may work on myself in between relationships, but I don't do as much work when I'm single compared to how hard I work when I have a partner. And what is all this bunk about waiting a year? Says who? Do you think someone is out there, perched on a chair with a daytimer, figuring out who is going to meet whom, and when, and, oops, this one better wait a few more months? Life is short. If I meet someone one day or five years after my last relationship, then that is when I'm meant to meet them.

I believe that we all long to be with someone, so why come out of a relationship where I've been miserable, and punish myself further by waiting on the sidelines of life for a year or more to pass just because that's what I am *supposed* to do? Not to say I haven't done it, I've gone years between relationships mostly because I haven't met someone. But I have also met someone soon after the end of a relationship and gotten involved right away. It really hasn't made much difference because I'm still me and I keep showing up in each relationship just the same, baggage and all, until, of course, I'm ready to change.

SOLUTION:

It's me who needs to change. When I find myself at that place *again*, that place where I've been hurt once more and I'm not letting others in, I have to do something to change my mind about the past. The past is over. I can choose to attract different experiences that will bring me different results.

When I find myself in that place of self sabotage, or beating myself up for the things I've done in the past, I reflect on my favourite Ernie Larson quote:

If nothing changes, nothing changes.

And I ask myself, what have I done that is different? What have I changed since the last time I was in this situation? Usually nothing but the colour of my hair! If nothing changes, nothing changes. It can't get much simpler than that. I have to be willing to *do* something, to take a step in the direction of my dreams.

I must be willing to do the work. So what is the work?

One of the agreements Shawn and I have made in our relationship is that at all times one of us is the adult. When one of us is living in the past and is riddled with old thoughts and fears, the other simply stays logical and doesn't buy into the fears at that point in time. Shawn's ex wife left him for someone else, so he sometimes struggles when I tell him I will not leave this relationship. When he's in a place of mistrust, I have to remember that his struggles are not mine, they are his. So I must be the adult and love him through his fear, which is just false evidence appearing real, and won't last long.

We all have fears. Sometimes we don't like to acknowledge how many fears we have packed into our bags, but we all have them. The more aware I am of the baggage I bring into this relationship, the better chance I will have at success.

We used to ask each other, "what's going on?" Then one day, Shawn told me he was changing the question to:

What are you afraid of right now?

This question cuts to the chase. When Shawn asks me what I'm afraid of right now, I am reminded to stop and think. I know I'm afraid of something and this question helps me get clear. "What's wrong?" shuts us both down. Sometimes I'm not clear about what's wrong right now and the question about fear takes me out of feeling sorry for myself and into solution.

Action Step:

Find a question that works for both of you instead of "what's wrong?" We use "what are you afraid of?" If it works for you, use it. If not, find a question that is non-threatening and easy to answer.

Ask your partner to support you in a way that works for you. For example, if you need space when you are struggling, ask for it. Don't shut your partner down, just ask for the support you need. Maybe you need a hug when you're in that place of fear. Talk about the type of support that works for you both, before you need it.

For a more detailed worksheet for this exercise, go to www.OliveJuiceForever.com

- Our baggage keeps us chained to the past, and limits our potential for happiness and success.

- Nothing will change, until I'm ready to change. And that means rolling up my sleeves and getting to work on ME!

- FEAR is false evidence appearing real.

- What am I afraid of right now?

OLIVE JUICE FOREVER

CHAPTER TWO

Power

So many couples spend so much time fighting for power — and nobody ever wins.

Take Jane and Tim. They were having some struggles in their marriage. Power struggles. By power, I mean they were fighting for control, trying to outdo each other in all areas of their marriage. Neither one of them was happy because each of them was always trying to influence the other's decisions and trying to win every argument.

Jane told me the grapefruit story. One morning, Tim was cutting a grapefruit for her and he was using a paring knife, not the grapefruit knife. She promptly *told* him that he was doing it wrong and that he should use a proper grapefruit knife, because it cuts the fruit closer to the skin and then you can slice all the sections nicely.

> I never knew there was such a thing as a grapefruit knife.

Shawn

I stopped her mid-sentence and asked, "Who cares what he cuts it with? He was cutting you a grapefruit. I wouldn't care if he was using a spoon or a piece of string, if my man wants to cut me a grapefruit that's enough for me."

"Hmmm," she said. "I get it."

I said, "If you want him to use a grapefruit knife, next time you cut a grapefruit, use the grapefruit knife and show him by example. *Show him by example.* Don't tell him you're showing him or teach him how to use it, *just use it.* And if the next time he uses a piece of string to cut your grapefruit just know that the grapefruit knife will still be sharp for you."

Power struggles create distance and hostility instead of closeness and trust. Power is a big word. Some people think it's a bad thing. I used to think power was about being in charge, about making all the decisions. And I always believed that it was the man who wielded all the power. My old definition of a powerful man was the boss, the one who took charge, looked after all the money. He was strong and demanding and when he spoke, everyone listened. A powerful woman, on the other hand, was controlling, bossy and hard to get along with.

Today I've changed my mind. I believe that a man or woman in power can be silent and still be powerful, that they know when to step up and they know when to step back and lead from behind. I think that people often mistake power for control.

Alison goes into paralysis when her husband drives because he always takes the long route. Then they end up in a big fight about which is the fastest way to go. The funny thing is, she's always complaining about not spending enough time with her husband because he's always working. Now he is driving (the long way) and they're fighting. Who's winning that one? And again, *who cares?* Who cares how they get there, just enjoy the journey.

The big question here is what do you want? Do you want to bicker and fight all the time? If so, carry on. If not, stop and ask yourself what do you really want to create for yourself? One of my favourite questions is:

Do I want to be right
or do I want to be happy?

I'm not suggesting that you don't speak up for yourself when something is bothering you, because then nobody is happy. The question is: do you need to be right about EVERYTHING? Or can you choose what's really important, speak your mind about those things and leave the rest alone? What I'm suggesting here is that you talk about issues as they come up. Talk all day if you need to. In fact, if you have a lot of issues together at this point, go away for the weekend and sort out as many as you can. Or make time each week to address a couple of issues. Resentment doesn't serve anyone by being bottled up inside, it ekes out in smart little comments, a look to kill, or an overreaction to something small. These are all ways that we fight for power in a relationship. And guess what? Nobody wins.

So if I'm always thinking he's out to get me, I'm watching every word I say and every action I take and at the same time watching him to see if I can catch him screwing something up so that I can be RIGHT. YES. RIGHT. What a feeling that is. It's like being in prison. I know it is, I did it for years. It got me nowhere but single and I was certainly not happy.

I can choose to play along in this struggle for power or I can choose to focus on what I want — which is to be happy.

All relationships are based on trust. My husband tells me that his intentions are always good and I believe him. I have to believe him if I want a loving, harmonious marriage. Both of us came into this relationship wounded in the area of trust and we have to continually earn each other's trust. We do this by keeping our word and by expressing our love for each other in lots of different ways.

SOLUTION:

TALK. TALK. TALK. TALK.

Our three-year-old son loves attention. Shawn and I each made up our minds years ago about the meaning of attention. In my family, we grew up singing and performing. I loved it, except for one experience. I was singing with all my cousins and apparently I was singing too loudly. I was told off in front of everyone and told I shouldn't be such a show off. Shawn had a totally different experience as a child; he was not encouraged to step into the limelight at all. Now we have this three-year-old who is trying to find his way in the world and I want him to "share" the stage and take turns because this is my way of protecting him while his dad is encouraging him all the more to get out there and perform.

This situation could have become a power struggle for Shawn and I over the next twenty years, but it won't because we talk about things. Once we understood each other's past experiences around seeking attention, it was easy to find a middle ground and find ways to give our son the attention he needs.

In our relationship I know that Shawn is my man and my protector. Part of protecting me is driving me places. Our car is his chariot and he is my hero. And he let me know right away that he is the boss in the bedroom. Great! When we go out for dinner he orders for me and I love it. I could spend all day looking at a menu and I am really not that fussy about what I eat. He can look at a menu and choose in minutes and I love that. At the grocery store checkout, he gives me his bank card to pay with. I have the same card from the same account but I like it when he pays and he gets to play the role of provider. It works for us. That's us. That's part of our big game. I love to be treated like a princess and he loves to play the prince. We both win and it isn't hurting anyone. His ego is being stroked and I get what I want. Each couple is going to be different so figure out what's important and make it work for you.

You know what? This is perfect for me. I get to enjoy and realize some traditional manly tasks in a relationship, like ordering dinner and driving us everywhere all the time. It's what I like to do.

I want to protect and care for Lorraine and she wants to be protected and be taken care of. I get my manly image/ego thing going on, and I get to take care of my woman. This is absolutely harmless stuff, and I get to feel good about these small contributions I make to our relationship.

Keep this one simple for the love of God. Pick your battles. Sort out what you really like to do, negotiate back and forth if you have to, and get on with it. Too much power either way is no good. Things are bound to go haywire.

I don't know. I'm just a guy.

Shawn

Shawn and I also have an agreement that neither of us will make a big decision without consulting the other. There are areas in our life where I wield more power. For example, I take care of all the money and kind of control our spending. This is how we've created balance in our relationship. We've each let go of the need to be right all of the time. We choose to focus on what works in our relationship, on the good evidence.

ACTION STEPS:

Take a piece of paper and make a list called "Five Things." Write down five or more things that you love or appreciate about your partner today. Look for evidence that your partner loves you. What did they do for you that you appreciated? What did they say? Take time to share what you have written, or put your list somewhere so your partner will see it, like on the fridge. If you have kids, do it for them, too.

Here are some examples:

- the great hug as you left this morning
- you cooked a great dinner
- we took the long way home, and I enjoyed it
- I love how you cut my grapefruit this morning
- the way you clapped when I was singing
- our family time at the park picnicking and playing ball

For a more detailed worksheet for this exercise, go to www.OliveJuiceForever.com

- Power struggles create distance and hostility instead of closeness and trust.
- Choose your battles wisely, not everything is worth fighting over.
- How do I love thee today, let me count the ways!
- Do I want to be right, or do I want to be happy?

CHAPTER THREE

Evidence

Do you walk the line? Do you ever hear people talk about living above or below the line?

Now, above the line is where happiness, integrity and freedom live. Above the line is where I get my olive juice: my love. When I live above the line, I am in control of my own destiny and it feels good. I love my life! When I am living above the line, I have goals, I know what they are, and I am moving in the direction of my dreams. I am accepting of life and work to keep living above the line by staying focused on what I want.

In the following story I was definitely living below the line.

I found out the man I was living with was having an affair and I was angry. Actually, I was furious. "How could you?" That was the question that I kept asking. "How could you do that to me? I was your friend. You knew how much I had been through and you promised me." He had promised, before we started dating, that if he ever wanted to be with another woman that he'd tell me first. We had known each other for years, so I was well aware of his promiscuous history. I blamed him but was angrier with myself because I knew. In my heart I already knew he was being unfaithful, and I was angry at myself more than anything for not listening to that voice inside that kept telling me: he's having an affair, he's having an affair. At the time, I had no physical evidence that he was fooling around and I didn't want to believe it, so I pretended to look for ways that he loved me instead. As much as I pretended to look for the love he was giving me, I was constantly listening for him to trip himself up so I could be right about him having an affair.

One thing I noticed was that he never put his phone down, it was always in his pocket on vibrate or silent and whenever it rang he would go out onto the deck. The day finally came when I couldn't play ignorant anymore. My ego was telling me to shut up and keep pretending. Things were good and what would people say and how could this have been happening. I teach this stuff for heaven's sakes. And on, and on, and on. In the moment that I acknowledged that he had been lying, I switched from a loving, caring, spiritual being to some kind of junkie looking for a fix.

I began my hurt hunt (as I call it) and I knew exactly where to go first. That f— phone was going to be my saving grace. I had filed his phone bills every month, never having looked at anything but the amount owed, and now they were going to be my proof. I couldn't get to that filing cabinet fast enough. I pulled out his cell phone bills and found exactly what I was looking for, the same number redialed over and over. I went to the phone, called the number and asked for her by name (I pretty sure I knew who it was). I found out she wasn't home and I hung up. I got to feel justified, I was right again. The evidence was building and in a sick and twisted way I was feeling good. My ego had taken over and I was now on a bit of a bender.

I was determined to take him out at the knees. That proof was a little jolt of righteous anger to help me feel better about myself. But it wasn't enough, my adrenalin was pumping and I was livid. More than that, I was hurt, devastated and I needed more proof. My insides were shaking so much that I couldn't keep any food down. That was okay, because my outsides were shaking so much I couldn't put food to my mouth. I did, however, manage to hang onto that phone bill.

Somehow I went back to that old place. I deserved this, how could I be such a fool not to know? Why did I get involved with a man who has had affairs all his life? It wasn't enough to know that he was having an affair. Now I had to know how long it had been going on. So I went back through the phone bills to see when it started.

It was as if I wasn't hurting enough and I needed to pull out the knife and stick it back in again. Once I found out when it started, I went looking for something else, the pain was deep but still not deep enough. How could I destroy him completely? What could I do now? Where else could I look? I went back to see what time of day he was calling her and noticed that often, our home number was called right after he called hers. I thought I would vomit when I saw how many times that had happened. I figured that they spent all their time having sex and laughing about what an idiot I must be. I tried to figure out his email account password because if I could have gotten into his hotmail account I would have. I tried every bloody word I could think of.

The intensity of the high I got from this hurt was so great that, when I came down, I just wanted another hit. So I started to make stuff up and boy am I good. He worked out of town half the time so I convinced myself that when he was working out of town, he was living with her. At some point during that afternoon, my 20-year-old daughter, Andrea, came home. I thought I was going insane. I couldn't keep still. I was pacing up and down and my heart was racing so much that I couldn't think straight. I was just so mad. I had no tears and that makes sense, as my mouth was so very dry. I am sure my body had gone into shock. Denial. Resistance. I wanted revenge. I had a plan.

I persuaded Andrea to call his workplace with a lie, to prove that he was lying to me about having to work the night of his birthday like he said he was. I got to be right about that too. I was very embarrassed that Andrea saw me that way but I was unstoppable. I was in shock, total reaction mode, as if something had taken me over. I knew what I was doing was wrong but somehow I couldn't stop.

He was working out of town that day, so when I had enough evidence, I got in his truck and drove to where he worked. As it happens, when I got there, he was washing and detailing my truck. I was choked because I had wanted to catch them in the act. He was surprised to see me, and he knew the gig was up. We went to a restaurant for dinner and I asked him if he was having an affair. He denied it so I asked him again. Once he admitted it, I felt like my life as I had known it was over. We had a great life, lived in the most glorious home, had a great family. In an instant it was all gone. I still didn't cry. I sat in shock listening to as many details as he was willing to disclose and then he drove me home. When I got home, in the comfort of my own bed, I cried. I cried and cried and cried. I didn't know where to turn. I was afraid.

Here's where I use the analogy of the line. I am either living above the line, finding love, or below the line, feeding fear. When I'm below the line, as in that story, I am resentful and vengeful. I get angry, I get even, and then I feel guilty and beat myself up because I really don't want to be a vengeful person. How many times have I been told to "rise above it?"

Well, when I'm hurting and looking for revenge, wanting you to hurt as much as me, it becomes a vicious cycle. I really end up hurting myself more than anyone else. Back then, I felt justified in continuing to paint him as the bad guy long after our relationship was over. The only person I was hurting was me. He was long gone, off with her or someone else. I was the only one still suffering.

Being angry is like drinking poison
and expecting someone else to die.

When I spend all my time convincing myself that men can't be trusted, I get to be even more right about it because now I look for it and see it everywhere and I continue to be the victim. Being a victim was easy for me. I had lived below the line a lot in my life, living the life of a victim and living it very well, I might add.

Living below the line becomes addictive: I get my love junkie fix there, my drama queen drive for intensity. It is unhealthy and a very unhappy place to be. It's where my ego lives and because my ego is protecting me, to keep me from looking stupid or embarrassed, it will do or say anything to keep me RIGHT, as opposed to happy.

The problem with living below the line is that, in a sick and twisted way, it feels good. I don't have to take any responsibility for any part of the situation because I am the victim and I feel justified in giving him what he deserves. In reality, it's a horrible place to be. It feels the shits and lots of people get to stay stuck in that for the rest of their lives. How do you get out of that cycle? Later in the book we will talk about the Big Game of Life, where you will find peace of mind. When you're clear about your goals, and your desire to reach a goal becomes bigger than the need to be right, you will start to move above the line.

The relationship in the above story didn't end right away. I knew that if I walked away without sorting out why I had attracted this into my life then, I would just repeat the pattern. As devastating as it all was — my ego was in crisis and my heart was broken — I still had that saving grace of knowing I had been right. Yes, I had known it all along. I knew it, I knew it, and I knew it. I recognized that all my life I had been saying, "Men can't be trusted," and all my life I had been proving myself right about that. So it made perfect sense to get involved with someone who had cheated for as long as he had been in relationships because I knew I was bound to prove myself right, somewhere along the line, AGAIN. Were these conscious thoughts? No. Can I look back over my life now and see where I kept trying to be right about men being untrustworthy? Yes. Was I happy? Absolutely not. Was I right? Yes.

So back to the big question: "Do I want to be right or do I want to be happy?"

Over the next few months I decided that I would change my mind. I started by asking myself the question:

What do I want?

And what I came up with was that I wanted to trust men and to attract a man who loves me and is trustworthy. Now, I know all the books say that I have to learn to trust myself first, but I know that I'm not going to fool around. It's him I'm unsure of. It doesn't serve me to disconnect myself from life and stay disconnected because I have been hurt over and over. I got really clear about what I wanted and started collecting evidence of it. I chose to not hang out with men who I know are untrustworthy. I surrounded myself with men who loved their partners. It was amazing, I began looking for stories of men who were loyal and loving and my pool of evidence grew and grew until I attracted a trustworthy partner of my own. I changed my mind and I changed my life.

SOLUTION:

I have come to trust that when my husband tells me that he loves me, he means it. I choose to trust him. He is an honest man and he adores me. Why would I not believe him? I have come to trust that when anyone tells me that they love me, they do. Why would I spend any more of my precious time questioning someone who genuinely loves me? Sometimes it's hard to let others in because we have been hurt in the past, but you know what? If we don't let others in, all we're doing is recreating that hurt for ourselves and for the person who is trying to love us. How sad it is when you love someone very much but you try to shut them out because of things that happened to you long ago.

It is so easy to say, "I've been hurt before and I am not letting myself get hurt again," or, "I had better not get too involved or give up to much of my heart in case he changes his mind about me." What happens if he really does love you, but you go to your grave still hanging onto a little piece of what if? Well let me tell you this — each and every day that I wake up and my husband tells me he loves me, I will cherish that day as if it were our last.

ACTION STEP:

Shawn reminds me often that his intentions are always good. Why go looking for evidence against that? Our solution to this hurt hunt is to leave evidence around that reminds us of our love and commitment to each other. For example, he married me and I am wearing a ring on my finger, that's a great reminder. Another piece of evidence is that when he leaves me notes around the house, I keep them and stick them on my PC or on my mirror and I am constantly reminded of how much he loves me. I do this because I love the feeling of finding a note; it is always a good reminder when I am feeling insecure, tired or afraid. We have a journal that we send to each other, we take turns writing in it and it's always there for us to read. We keep cards we've sent each other in a special box, and have a family wall that includes recent pictures of us.

What kind of evidence do you have in your home? In your purse or pocket? Car? What about your desk at work? What do you have that reminds you of the love you have for each other and the commitment to your life together?

Create a notes-to-each-other journal and take turns jotting down thoughts and messages to each other. It doesn't have to be daily or even weekly. Do it when you want to cherish a moment or remind each other of how much love you share. Write about great dates you go on or keep it as simple as a conversation that you want to remember.

Dig out that box of photos, put them into an album. Pick your favourites, frame and hang them where you can both see them. Dust off those love letters and re-read them. Start looking at your life with new eyes, and find the good evidence, it's there.

On our website at www.OliveJuiceForever.com you'll find an exercise on finding good evidence. We had fun creating this worksheet and we hope you enjoy your treasure hunt together.

- We are always experiencing one of two emotions: fear or love.

- I am either living below the line, in fear, or above the line, in love.

- Being angry is like drinking poison and expecting someone else to die.

- What do I want?

CHAPTER FOUR

Forgiveness

I was sixteen years old, lying in a hospital bed after being in a horrific car accident. My back was broken and I had a lot of other injuries including a punctured lung. I was on oxygen and for a long time I was so drugged up I had no idea where I was. One thing I did know was that I deserved to be hurt that badly.

For many years, I didn't believe I deserved to have a good life. In fact I didn't believe I deserved to have any life. I thought I deserved the suffering that came from that accident, as I had aborted a child just months before, and the emotional pain was almost killing me. The guilt I carried was so great that the physical injuries were not only a relief, but minimal compared to the suffering of my soul. As I lay there fighting for my life people were feeling sorry for me and I couldn't understand it. "I deserved this," I wanted to yell. But I couldn't speak and lay there consumed with guilt. At the same time I began to enjoy the attention I was getting for being such a heroic victim.

Living the life of a victim served me well. It was easy, I didn't have to do much. Well, not that much, just tell my story one hundred and one different ways so people would react with, "Well, no wonder, you poor little dove," or, "I'm surprised you've made it this far." Then, with all their support, I didn't have to do anything else because I was now a hero just for being a survivor.

Hero or not, I was still angry and unable to forgive myself. One side of me was crying out for love and affection while the other side wouldn't allow me to have it. I attracted abusive relationships and became addicted to drugs and alcohol, hurting myself more and more all the time, and still it wasn't painful enough. I didn't believe I deserved to be happy so I did whatever I could to punish myself.

Why was I so angry? Was it that I just didn't trust enough, or that I simply didn't believe that I deserved to have a happy life? Why am I so complicated? Why did I still feel the need to punish myself? Am I alone? I don't think so. The world is so full of hurt and shame that it's understandable that there is so much pain and suffering. Why did I continue to beat myself up? How did I end my suffering?

Stop. Just stop.

I had to stop hurting myself. Nobody can hurt me like I hurt myself, or say such cruel things as I say to myself, and certainly not as often. Nobody can take away my power; I give my power away. So why did I continue to beat myself up over and over again?

When is enough, enough?

Suffering is unnecessary, unwise and uncomfortable. So why does it feel so good to sit and dwell in the yuck? Is it because it's familiar? Why do we waste what little time we have on this earth worrying about things that have already happened? It's in the past. It's done. It's out of our control. Why did I continue to look for ways to hurt myself? I got caught up in that cycle of living below the line. The person I was so angry at was me. Don't get me wrong, I blamed everyone else, but it was me I was angry at.

At one point in my life I was in a treatment center. I was so ashamed of the person that I had become and the things I had done. Someone asked me, "Do all these things that have happened to you, and that you are ashamed of, have a name?" "Yes, of course, abuse, rape, adultery, addiction, rage." He said, "If they have a name, it means that someone else has also experienced them."

That gave me some hope. I realized that I wasn't alone and if I wanted to begin the journey to self love, then this was a good place to start.

SOLUTION:

Studies have been done to determine the impact of exercise, healthy eating, smoking, drinking and various other stress factors on health and longevity. The major finding was that all things we normally expect to impact on health were not the most significant determinants: attitudes of gratitude and forgiveness are the key factors in positively influencing health.

I had to forgive myself. Easier said than done.

I started by learning how to be just a little compassionate with myself. I have listened to many stories over the years and have always felt great compassion and understanding for others and their journeys. Why not give myself the same courtesy? Have you read or heard these words before?

> *Forgive us our trespasses, as we forgive*
> *those who trespass against us.*

I had to learn to forgive myself. I started by forgiving others for the hurts that I had endured at their hand. I had to forgive people for not being there for me when I needed them and I had to forgive myself for not asking for help when I so desperately needed it. And I had to forgive myself for the things I had done.

I have done what I have done in order to survive. What I know about my life today is, had I not experienced all that pain and suffering, I wouldn't know all the love I have today.

Action Step:

How do we go from hurting ourselves to loving ourselves?

As easily as answering the question, "How shall I eat this elephant?"

One bite at a time.

Write a letter to yourself about something from your past that you feel sad or angry about. Read it out loud, either to yourself or your partner and then decide to let it go. Burn it, rip it up, but get rid of it. You don't need to hang onto it any longer.

Now write another letter. Write a story about the relationship you want to have with yourself and the people in your life. Read that one out loud and keep it close, read it everyday.

For more detailed instructions on how to write these letters, go to www.OliveJuiceForever.com

- If it has a name, someone else has experienced it.

- I must learn to forgive myself and let the past go.

- Suffering is unwise, unnecessary and uncomfortable.

- Attitudes of gratitude and forgiveness are the key factors in positively influencing health.

- How shall I eat this elephant? *One bite at a time.*

PART TWO

TODAY

CHAPTER FIVE

Image

The other day I watched our three-year-old twins play make believe. He, Johnny Cash with his guitar, was confessing his love to his little sister, June Carter…they were laughing and having a great time, and were right into their game until they saw me watching, and then they got embarrassed and stopped.

I don't know why they stopped, as their Dad and I play Johnny and June all the time. Shawn has a black guitar that he has no idea how to play, and I have a tambourine. When Shawn announced in front of about 150 people that we had just gotten married, we were dressed like Johnny and June, me in my beautiful June Carter Cash dress and he was all in black with cufflinks that have "Johnny" engraved on them. We play the *Walk the Line* CD and sing "We got Married in a Fever," and we love it. We don't pretend to be them all the time but we will sometimes sign notes to each other from Johnny or June Bug and I often call him "my Johnny." It is fun, freeing and harmless.

We don't think many of our adult friends act this way. Maybe they do, but if they do they don't talk about it. But you know what? They all love it. It came out quite by accident that we play this game and ever since then, people have been approaching us and saying, "we love what you do and we want to create more fun in our lives." GREAT, that's wonderful, play, have fun, look foolish….

Look foolish? What will the neighbours say?

As children learning to walk, we fall down, get up, fall down, and get up again. We laugh and we cry, but we don't give up, we keep trying until we get it. Then we learn to talk, and to ride a bike, and we don't care what we look like or if we don't get it right away, we just keep trying.

Then somewhere along the line something happens. Someone makes fun of us or gets angry at us for not getting it "right," and something changes. As we get older we seem to be a little less adventurous, and start to give up faster when it comes to learning something new.

We spend the rest of our lives protecting an image we have created for ourselves, and to protect that image we stop participating, because we may look stupid, and then the fun is gone. We stop trying new things in case we can't get it right the first time, and we start measuring ourselves against others.

We look around and compare our outsides: the cars we drive and the houses we live in, the size of our butts and boobs, but what about the insides, our feelings of self worth and deservability? It's easy to sit and chat with friends about the new car or home you're buying, but to say I'm feeling sad and lonely is kind of pathetic. We weren't born with owners' manuals, yet we're expected to be all fixed and perfect, both inside and out. Where the heck were we supposed to learn all of this?

I believe we have all been boxed into what society says is acceptable. Who is society? Who wrote the rules? Who makes the decisions? We are afraid of speaking our minds and saying the wrong thing in case we look stupid. We take on two jobs to make more money to buy more stuff, so everyone will think we've got it all together. We read airbrushed magazines and see these anorexic women, who we then want to emulate. Then we beat ourselves up because we don't look like them. It gets even worse as we watch our partners, the ones who love us "just the way we are," gawk over a beautiful woman in our presence and then want us to get naked later. We spend money we don't have at Christmas and we tell the ones we love that we love them on Valentine's Day because we're supposed to. And then we wonder why our self esteem is in the toilet.

Good grief! I don't stand a chance — who does? Lack of self esteem is rampant in our society and we wonder why? I don't know one person who isn't affected by low self esteem, and smart marketers are forever reminding us with the products they sell that we are getting older, fatter and balder. Well, thank goodness they have all the products we could ever need to remedy those failings: pills and vitamins, thickening shampoos, running shoes, wrinkle reducing creams, cream you rub on your butt and the fat disappears and on and on it goes.

What about a bottle of "I love you just the way you are" perfume instead of all the pretentious names they come up with? Our self esteem is already trashed, and someone, somewhere, will try to make us feel better by emphasizing our imperfections. If we weren't trying to be what we thought everyone else wanted us to become, then we wouldn't need all that stuff that we keep buying. Then we wouldn't need extra income and we might even have more time to spend doing the things we want to do with the people we love.

I believe we are born whole and complete beings, full of love, each of us totally unique. One day, early in our lives, something happens and we realize that we aren't the same as everyone else and our uniqueness is not okay. We think somehow that in order to be accepted for who we are, we have to clone ourselves after everyone else.

So we start to give our power away so that we will be more accepted by society. Then we realize we don't know who we are anymore, so we go on a quest to rediscover just who we are. Is that really what life is all about?

We crave acceptance and love. That's why we start to give ourselves up early. We start with our parents. We want to please them so much, we do the things they want us to do and end up giving up a piece of ourselves. Then we move onto school and give up even more. We look for the most popular kid and emulate them to a point where we start to lose track of ourselves, who we are and how we think, what we say and how we dress. Once we fall in love it's over. Some of us become whoever we think our partner wants us to be, even though it was "us" they fell in love with before we changed for them.

Maybe this isn't you, but it certainly was me. By the time I was 16, I had no idea who I was and what I stood for. I became a shell of a young woman, standing on the sideline of the game of life, wanting so badly to be on the team, but what team? What sport? I had given up so much of my identity already that I was afraid to choose a team or to be on the field. What if I chose the wrong thing, what if I wasn't good enough and sat on the bench, how would that look? I was afraid and didn't feel as if I would do any team any good, so I sat and watched and started to give up my passion for life until I just wanted to end it. In trying to be perfect, to please everyone all the time, I did nothing.

I read recently that if I say I know how to do something but I'm not doing it, then I don't really know it and have only heard about it. How true is that? I am so fast to say, "Oh, I know that," but do I? Am I doing it? If I am not doing it then I don't know it, I have only heard about it.

What's wrong with saying "I don't know?" Or, "I need help?" Nobody taught me how to be a wife or a mother or a great lover. I had to figure it all out by myself. I went to school and learned the names of all 50 U.S. states and their capitals and I learned about scalene triangles, but nobody taught me how to handle my internal stress monitor when my baby was screaming or how to really listen to what someone is saying.

There are some things that I think we are supposed to know instinctively, like parenting and being married. Yes, we have mentors, like our parents, but how many of us grow up saying I am never going to be like that and wonder how it came to be that that's exactly how we turned out. How did our parents learn to become parents? We all do our best but we haven't been given any tools to work with, so how are we supposed to know what to do?

A few years ago, I went to the SPCA to adopt a dog. The staff had to send someone out to my home to check it out before they would release the dog into my care. I thought that was great until a few months later my daughter had a baby and nobody came to see where that baby was going to be living. Something is missing here....

Why, oh why, when there is so much goodness and beauty surrounding us, do we focus on what is not good? How many people sit around their workplace celebrating the opportunities that they have there, that their job provides an opportunity to feed their families and house and clothe them? And if someone did that, the rest of the crew would think they were crazy. Instead, I hear a lot of people tell me that they hate their jobs and they focus on what the company is out to do to them and not for them. Our society has become so engrossed in what everyone is "doing to me" that we have lost track of what we're here for and what we can do for others. The fight to the top is so consuming that I am not surprised there is no trust in the world.

How many parents play at the park with their kids? I took our children to gymnastics one day and told them I was going to jump on the trampoline or walk along the balance beam and do some cartwheels. They were quick to say, "You can't do that, you're an adult." I have to sit and watch because parents don't play. My sisters and I always put on shows when we were growing up and always played dress up. My parents' home has a spiral staircase and we still go over and have fashion shows. My Mum finds dresses at the Salvation Army or some little second hand store and brings them home and washes them up and we wear them. I got married in a ten dollar dress that my mum found for me. You know it's a good dress if it costs ten dollars, and I'm proud of it. We still sing together and put on shows; we all get together and play games. I think people have become way too serious and have forgotten how to have fun.

One day, I was driving home with the kids and we were all singing together. I have privacy windows so anybody driving by couldn't see that I had three-year-old twins in the back seat and that we were all singing. I stopped at the lights and was clapping and singing, and out of the corner of my eye something caught my attention. I looked over into the next vehicle and here was this man singing and clapping away and having a great time, until he saw me watching, then he stopped and looked totally embarrassed. I gave him the biggest smile and kept on singing and clapping. What a shame that he had to be embarrassed about having fun and getting caught having fun. I don't know about you but I am at my happiest when I get to share in someone else's joy and happiness. I am mesmerized watching kids play and laugh. Why do we think it's all kids' play and that there is no room for us to have fun, too?

Studies show that laughter is a major factor in longevity, so why don't we focus on creating more humor in our lives? A child laughs an average of 200-250 times a day compared to adults who come in at 15-20 times a day. Something to think about, wouldn't you say?

SOLUTION:

As important as it is for Shawn and I to create time for intimacy, we also need to create time to play and laugh. How do we do that? We create monthly romantic dates for each other and they are exciting, but we also choose one day a month to be our free day. We do whatever we want that day, and it's always good for a laugh. Setting that free day and planning our dates has become paramount, because life gets in the way and just like anything else it can all get way too serious, and we forget what's most important to us.

I see and hear people worry about the things they can't change, like other people for example. People worry about what others are doing and being and saying and are so preoccupied by all this that they end up not showing up as themselves in case somebody else doesn't like it. We are all different. We are unique human beings, each with a different part to play in this world, so why do we try and take on the roles of others? For so long I didn't even know who I was. I tried so hard to match my insides to other people's outsides. I'm not other people. Throughout my life, I have tried to downplay my energy and enthusiasm in case other people wouldn't understand or couldn't keep up or would feel threatened by my desires to be, do and have so much. Well, not any more. I know that the past is the past and it is time to live in today, in my own unique way.

When we pretend that we have no issues or everything is okay we are kidding ourselves, our partners and the rest of the world. Or maybe we are just kidding ourselves because others can see through us, especially those we love the most. You might as well come clean and get some support around whatever it is that's up for you.

I've tried to protect my image from some of the things I've done in my life. Protect it to the point that I forgot who I was.

It's tiring, trying to maintain a facade of a man living in integrity, when I was packing around so much shame. The protection of my ego, "I'm the man," stopped me from moving forward, taking risks, reaching my potential and showing up as who I really am. The shame associated with my past kept me hidden and under the radar for so many years. I kept hoping that I would reach my goals and dreams quietly, without exposure or ridicule.

I have worked so hard over the last 12 years to be a man of integrity and loyalty, fighting to regain those virtues that I once had and lost.

I know that all I've ever wanted was love and acceptance in my life, from family, friends, or the women in my life, but I didn't know how to accomplish those things in a positive way, so I didn't.

How do I determine whether or not I'm done paying the price for my past?

I understand today that by showing up in life as who I really am, the more open to love and acceptance I'm able to be. What a freaking concept. Who knew? And I get way more loving and acceptance than I have ever had.

Shawn

Let's teach our kids that it's okay to not know everything and that it's okay to ask for help. Let's take our kids to the gas station and ask for directions to the park instead of missing their ball game because we think we can find it ourselves.

ACTION STEP:

Take little pieces of paper and write down some crazy or wonderful things that you would like to do together but have never done because you didn't think you could. Fold them up and put them in a cup. Choose one and go do it.

Here are some examples:

- go sing karaoke or take dancing lessons
- splash around the local fountain or play at the park
- buy a kite and learn to fly it
- take skydiving or scuba lessons
- go on a healing retreat or learn about tantric sex
- spend an afternoon together at your favourite book store or coffee shop

- get those season tickets or front row seats you've been wanting for years
- redo your bedroom into a sensuous or tranquil retreat

For a more detailed worksheet for this exercise, go to www.OliveJuiceForever.com

☾ We are born whole and complete beings, full of love, each of us totally unique.

☾ Children laugh 20 times more than adults, everyday. Let's get back to having fun!

☾ Why are our butts, boobs and bank accounts more important that our hearts, heads and self worth?

CHAPTER SIX

Needs

In astrology, I am a Sagittarian. I am a female. In my family of origin I am the first born. Myers Briggs says I am an ENFP, and according to Dan Millman's book, *The Life You Were Born to Live*, I am a number 5. Pamala Oslie's book, *Life Colors*, tells me I am a green/ violet and in the Chinese horoscope, I am an ox. Now, that's all very exciting and it's easy for me to justify some of my behaviour by saying "Well, I'm a Sagittarian, so what do you expect." But those categories and labels don't help me change.

Needs, needs, needs. We all have them, just ask Abraham Maslow. Maslow's famous hierarchy puts our needs into five basic categories.

Imagine a pyramid divided into five levels. At the base, the foundation is level 1, our biggest needs, physiological needs like oxygen, water and food, sleep, sex and avoiding pain.

Moving up, level 2 covers the need for safety and security like a home, money, stability and some order in life. Next, level 3 deals with the need for love and belonging, needs like family, spouse and community.

Level 4 is esteem needs, where Maslow defines two kinds of esteem needs, a lower and a higher one. The lower one is the need for the respect of others, the need for status, fame, glory, recognition, attention, reputation, appreciation, and dignity, even dominance. The higher form involves the need for self-respect, including such feelings as confidence, competence, achievement, mastery, independence, and freedom.

In the first two levels of Maslow's hierarchy, physiological and safety, the needs are really basic; we all have these same needs. Once you move up to the third and fourth levels, the needs become more individual, more unique to each of us, they define who we are at our core.

Like a painter, we all have our own customized palette of colours that we choose to create our canvas of life. There's a huge difference between a painting by Monet or van Gogh, even though they both use the same basic colours. I may choose some of the same colours as the next person, but the way I mix and use them defines me. You and I may have the same list of needs but we will get them met differently.

Maslow calls the first four levels deficit needs. I'd heard about his theory for years but didn't really understand it until I took a series of self development programs. There I learned about deficit needs, and how I am driven to satisfy these needs. As essential to me as paint to the artist, I am *always* getting them met, whether constructively or destructively.

The negative version of these needs shows up as low self esteem, inferiority complexes, addictions and unfulfilled lives. Maslow felt that these were at the root of many, if not most, of our psychological problems.

What I know now is when I am getting my driving needs met constructively, I move closer to level 5, at the top of the pyramid: self actualization. Self-actualization doesn't involve balance, once engaged it continues to be felt. This is the continuous desire to fulfill potentials, to be all that I can be, which is why it's called self actualization.

We can identify or label our driving needs with words or phrases that resonate for us, that show our true colours. I would love to have nice gentle words like harmony, creativity and nurturing but I don't. My list includes challenge, intensity, attention, and autonomy. I know what they are because I'm always striving to satisfy them.

Let's take challenge for a start. I can and do get challenge met destructively by waiting until the last minute to get ready to go somewhere. When I come out looking and smelling like a rose I've met my challenge in that I beat the clock. This is not always constructive, as I get flustered and agitated and a bit grumpy, not exactly the experience I am looking for (nor those around me). When I'm celebrating destructive behaviour I know that I'm not getting challenge met constructively. To get my need for challenge met constructively doesn't mean that I have to run a marathon every day or go bungee jumping. I can set myself up to unload the dishwasher before the kettle comes to a boil, or set my alarm for fifteen minutes and see if I can clean up six things on my desk.

If you want to find a quick and destructive way to get your needs met, choose addiction. Any addiction. Drinking and drugging are great ways to get challenge and freedom met destructively. A workaholic gets accomplishment met destructively by working every waking minute and not creating balance in their lives for their families, health and fun. Overeating can be a way to satisfy a need for attention or control. Intimacy can easily be met destructively in affairs.

> I crave intimacy. Doesn't sound very manly, I know.
>
> Picture this: we're lying on a sheep skin rug in front of a roaring fire, in a beautiful log cabin, sipping Grand Marnier, wearing wool sweaters, the snow is falling softly on the roof top, and we're listening to freakin' Barry White. No, that's not my definition of intimacy.
>
> How I used to get intimacy in my life was through alcohol, women and drugs. I found some very creative and unhealthy ways to get love and acceptance, and it was great.

73

But you know what? When I was in that lifestyle, I didn't know what I know today, I just knew I was dying inside. My self worth was in the toilet. Lying, hurting, cheating, I would've done anything, and almost did, to get my needs for intimacy and acceptance met.

My craving to get those needs met was so much stronger than the guilt and remorse associated with it. So much so, that the next day, I'd go out and do it all over again.

I was a love junkie looking for my next fix.

Shawn

Now I clearly own challenge, intensity, attention, and autonomy as my driving needs. They are cool things to be. But I didn't want to admit that maybe intimacy was a need for me. It's a bit of a fluffy word and I don't consider myself fluffy. Girls like that stuff and I know I am a girl but I would rather be writing a book than cutting out paper hearts. In my dictionary, intimacy is rather a weak word because it is a matter of the heart and I've not always done that well with matters of the heart. I may have a good head for business and coaching but not love stuff.

What I've come to understand is that my driving needs are mine, I can't pick and choose them, I have to make do with what I've got. And, guess what? Intimacy is one of my needs. Not only that, it's the biggest one, love junkie that I am. What does that mean and how come it's so important? Why do you think people get involved in affairs or get drunk in order to open up to others? I don't think we intentionally set out to do those things. I think that we long for companionship and are looking for someone to feed that part of us that is starving, that piece of us that we don't always want to admit to having. It seems weak to want or need others so we pretend it doesn't exist. But it does exist. And for many of us it exists in a BIG way.

Why do you think I became involved with cell phone man? I had known him as a friend for years, and I knew his history of infidelity. So what drove me to get involved with him? I was not getting my need for intimacy met anywhere else. I walked in with my eyes wide open, asking myself, "why am I doing this?" This was before I really understood how my driving needs can run my life. Deep down I knew getting into this relationship wasn't the right thing to do, but I couldn't stop myself.

If you ever find yourself picking fights more than usual, it could be because you aren't getting your need for intimacy met constructively. In picking fights it's getting met, but destructively. It takes seconds to pick a fight but it takes hours to cook a candlelight dinner. Which is easier? Hours to cook dinner or seconds to start a fight? You certainly get intimacy met in fighting. Once you get that fix from fighting, it becomes habit and then it becomes comfortable. Learning this was huge in my journey through self development and I continue to ask myself daily, "What need am I getting met right now?" Now that I am aware of my needs, I really enjoy looking for ways to get them met constructively.

SOLUTION:

The only solution here for me was to take the time to figure out what my needs are, and it's a continual process. It certainly doesn't take up all my time scheduling how I'll get them met, but I do ask myself, especially when I'm behaving destructively, "Which of my needs am I meeting now?"

First thing I did was attract a man who has a need for intimacy as big as my own. We have all kinds of constructive ways to get intimacy met together and, very importantly, we do not expect each other to fill those needs for us. It's healthy for me to find ways to create intimacy inside and outside of my relationship. The time that I spend alone writing in silence is very intimate to me and my cup is full before Shawn comes home at the end of the day. If I sat here waiting for him to come home and fill that need, it would put a huge pressure of expectation on him.

I had to get clear on what drives me and I had to be willing to do the work to change the behaviours that weren't working. It's about awareness more than anything, and once I became aware of my destructive behaviours it was easier to figure out when I was acting out. Finding solutions has become fun. In going from destructive to constructive, I was able to move from below the line to above the line and feel better about myself.

ACTION STEP:

Choose a situation that comes up in your life regularly. It could be being late, always speeding, overspending or arguing over nothing. What you could be getting out of this behaviour?

Let's look at speeding. This is clearly destructive behaviour, breaking the law, putting your life and the lives of others at risk, etc. As a driving need, this could be described by any number of words or phrases: challenge, risk, intensity, excitement. If you speed, pick or find a word that resonates for you. If it's challenge, think about how you might meet that need constructively. Learning to fly, rock climbing, or scuba lessons come to mind.

Go to our website at www.OliveJuiceForever.com and print off the worksheet that will help you get closer to determining your individual needs.

- Whether we know it or not, we all have unique needs that drive us to do the things we do.

- We are always getting our needs met, constructively or destructively.

- To start understanding your driving needs, look at recurring situations in your life.

- What are your driving needs?

CHAPTER SEVEN

Choice

At any given time I am in one of two places: fear or love.

Webster's dictionary says:

fear an unpleasant, often strong emotion caused by expectation or awareness of danger

love strong affection

fear profound reverence to God

love to feel a passion, devotion or tenderness for

My personal dictionary says:

fear keeps me stuck

love motivates me

fear is constricting, dark and dismal

love is a beautiful, freeing feeling

fear paralyzes

love propels

81

I find it sad that people want to have faith, faith in God, life, our countries, our leaders, each other, and ourselves. Yet it is those very things, religion, politics, schools, families, the media, life, each other and ourselves that are forever reminding us that being alive is fearful.

Lock your doors or someone might break in. Don't speak to strangers or you might be harmed. Eat all your vegetables to prevent cancer. Do your homework so you won't fail. Pray so God will be good to you. Be nice so others won't be mean. Don't look in case it's scary. Look in case you miss something. Sit up straight so you don't ruin your posture.

As I have said, you can only be living in one of two places: fear or love.

Think about any feeling that you have and ask yourself: am I in fear or love? There are varying degrees of fear and love, but it is only one or the other. My degree of love can go from feeling content to ecstatic, or my fear from edgy to rage. When I'm above the line, living in love, I'm okay to be where I am, I'm happy. But when I'm in that place of fear, it seems to grow rapidly, escalating from a mustard seed into some great big worldwide event, like making a mountain out of a molehill.

I recently had an experience of self perpetuating fear. I was paying the bills and looked at our visa statement and saw a charge for a hotel in a different city. I immediately froze. "Oh no," I thought, "not this again." Back in chapter three when I was scouring those cell phone bills I found a hotel listed on my visa statement, a hotel I had not visited. When I was living in chapter three, I had just found out my partner was having an affair. The additional evidence that he had spent the night with her at a fancy lodge on the west coast was enough to send me way below the line, to a place where as I was very angry and very, very afraid.

Back to the present and I am experiencing the same feeling: fear. I immediately started looking for more evidence on our visa statement, and found another hotel, this one in our hometown. I felt gutted and my first reaction was to become even more afraid, and then my thoughts turned to "someone is using our credit card fraudulently." Then I realized that Shawn had used our credit card to set up hotel rooms for some of his staff. I was right and I was happy. This entire process took less than two minutes.

I was happy I hadn't reacted as I would have done in the past, resenting and raging before I thought things through. Even though I know how much Shawn loves me, it still didn't stop me from reacting when I was afraid. My warrior woman's protective armor wants to keep me safe from any more hurt. Fear creates reaction and love creates response.

React or respond. When I am afraid, stuck in image, not wanting to be wrong, I will react to a situation. I could have reacted to the above story by spiraling into my fear and poor Shawn would've come home to a crazy woman and all he did was pay for a room for one of his staff with his credit card. Luckily I responded by taking my time to think the situation through, looking for the evidence that he is with me and not against me, and I found it.

Shawn and I have created a relationship built on trust; this relationship is so strong that it was ridiculous to think that he would be fooling around. Absolutely ridiculous, therefore, I didn't stay in that place of fear, I immediately moved above the line into a much healthier space: love. That felt so good.

You become what you think
about most of the time.
Ralph Waldo Emerson

Fear begets fear. What are you thinking about? What are you afraid of now? What do you do when you're in fear and you don't want to be there anymore?

How do we move from fear to love?

I have come to believe that there is a cycle that is prevalent among many of us. We want to be loved and crave intimacy and yet we are afraid to show up completely as ourselves because we don't think others will love us just the way we are. Many of us were taught that loving ourselves is selfish and arrogant or we came to believe somewhere along our paths that we weren't worthy of love.

We carry on with our lives trying to be who we think others will love, giving up all authenticity and never achieving the intimacy we are craving because we are not real. This is so frustrating and causes so much pain, as we try to find self love through loving someone else.

How many people really believe they are unlovable? Lots. I have been there and seen it over and over and over again: they believe that if they find someone who loves them, only then will they be happy and filled with love.

Wouldn't that be great, none of us would have to do any work except find someone to do everything to make us happy and in exchange, all we would have to do is the same for them? Whew…after a while it would get kind of tiring and especially when most people forget to ask the other what it is that makes them happy in the first place. If I don't love myself and this person is out there busting their butt to make me happy, chances are they aren't going to succeed because I probably don't even know what it takes to make me happy.

It doesn't work that way. I can't experience any more love for another than I have for myself. Everyone in my life can love me and love me and love me but until I learn to love myself their love will not be felt by me. If I don't love myself I certainly am not going to have the kind of relationship that I have been craving all these years.

SOLUTION:

How can I let the love in?

This is where faith comes in and I have to take a step. In order to feel their love I have to love myself. And in order for me to love myself I have to love another. When I could start to see the good in others it seemed okay to find it in myself.

A friend of mine gave me one of my greatest gifts when he said, "If I could give you a gift, it would be that you see yourself the way that others see you." WOW.

That sure hit home. I have passed that one along many times since.

So what can we do? We must do something. Take a step of faith, it doesn't have to be a leap, but take a step.

When a former partner died, I was so afraid and in so much pain that I never thought I could love again and I totally shut myself down. The day of his funeral, surrounded by friends and family, I experienced more love than I had ever known in my life. Yet, there I was ten months later, still sitting on the sidelines of life. I wouldn't see anyone or go anywhere. I was deep in fear.

I knew then I was at a crossroads and I had to make a decision. It would be easy to stay in that place of victim, alone and "safe," to just give up and let my life carry on until I died. Or I could pull myself out of that dark cave of isolation by going and doing something for others. I decided I had to take a leap of faith.

To get my life back I decided to give back, so I took a job in a detox centre in the Downtown Eastside, the rough part of Vancouver, B.C. As I became more compassionate with others, I became more compassionate with myself. By loving others I was able to start building some love for myself.

ACTION STEP:

Go do something, anything, for someone else. It could range from the simple, holding a door or making a special meal, to mowing your elderly neighbour's lawn or volunteering somewhere for a day, a week or longer. Connect with someone you haven't seen in a while. Give without expectation of return.

For a more detailed worksheet for this exercise, go to www.OliveJuiceForever.com

- At any given time, we are in one of two places: fear or love.

- Fear begets fear, love begets love.

- We become what we think about most of the time.

- How can I move from fear to love?

CHAPTER EIGHT

Love

I have learned over and over that we are here for two reasons: to serve and to love. Pretty simple, wouldn't you say? Wouldn't it be great if we all started our days being grateful for the opportunity to be of service and to always practise love?

I was at a conference some years ago where a man named Frank told a story that has stayed with me all these years. I have also practised it many times. The story goes like this:

Frank was in a prison talking to the prisoners and telling his story. At the end of the story he finished the way he always did by saying "has anyone told you that they love you yet today? And if not, let me be the first to say 'I love you'." Well, as usual people came up to say thanks and as he was surrounded by men, this big, angry-looking man pushed his way to the front and with tears in his eyes he asked Frank if what he had said was true. Frank replied by saying that it was all true and asked which part he meant in particular. The angry-looking man responded by saying "the I love you part." Nobody had ever said "I love you" to him, ever. He was clearly touched by those words. What a great gift both he and Frank received that day.

In this story Frank touched that man's heart in a way that both of them will never forget. Love and compassion are two of the greatest gifts we have to give. So why do we hold back? Why do we think that we have to wait for someone to say "I love you" before we say it back? Why do I count the nice things you do for me before I do something back. Do we really need to keep it even? By doing something nice for you I am rewarded with a feeling of love, so why do I even need you to do anything for me? I don't need you to do anything for me, *but you'd better.*

Why? Because we have been taught that things always have to be fair? That's great but why do we give so much and then stop because we aren't getting anything back? I am not talking about "material" stuff here. I could be, but I am talking about the "love" stuff. If I am holding your hand and everyday I am the one to reach out to hold your hand, after a while I might start to think "well, maybe he doesn't want to hold my hand, so I am just going to wait until he holds mine," which is living below the line. Maybe he is so used to me putting my hand out to hold his, that he doesn't think of it and next thing you know I am making up that he doesn't want to be seen with me in public and then he doesn't love me and on and on and on it goes. Can anyone relate to this or is it just me?

Maybe it's not that important for him to hold hands in public and maybe he is thinking about something special he is going to do for me later, or maybe he is thinking about the game on TV. If I want to hold his hand, then I reach out and take it. Whether I am reaching out for my husband's hand or he mine, the feeling is the same when we connect: love.

We don't do great things,
only small things with great love.

Mother Theresa

My husband replaces my soap in the shower when mine is dissolving. He does this as an act of love. When I get into the shower and see that new bar of soap I feel special. That feeling of love and appreciation feels so good. My point here is that we aren't even in the same room and yet we both feel the love. How do you feel when you are writing a card to a loved one, donating to a charity, throwing someone a party, preparing food for others?

What about when we are hurting? Whether we have had a fight or are feeling beaten up about life, what do we do then? I tend to shut down and don't let anyone in, which doesn't help me at all because that is when I am needing love the most, either from myself or others. And I don't usually feel that great about myself when I am feeling down and out, so turning to the mirror isn't always the best answer.

Sometimes I just need to call a friend. Sometimes I call and sometimes I don't. Maybe I don't call because hurting that bad feels good, and then I can punish the person who is hurting me by letting them see how much I am hurting. I'll show you. I know people who are so bitter that they stay there for years, dying the valiant fight by being angry for their whole lives. You can see it on some people's faces, in their body language, in their actions.

What about when my loved ones are hurting? Even when I am angry and hurting I have come to know that the best thing I can do is remember that I love them anyway. It doesn't serve either of us to continue to punish each other, but this is where that ego comes in again and we want to continue to be right. How long will this fight last and how much time and energy do I want to give to the negative feelings?

So I ask myself:

Do I want to be right or
do I want to be happy?

If the answer is I want to be happy, then I ask the second question:

What would love do here?

95

When my guy is going through feelings of hurt or rejection and I don't know how to support him, I ask myself "how would I want to be supported right now?" Would I want a hug or some space? Usually I would love a hug but not always know how to ask for it, especially when I am hurting. If I believe that in loving him I am loving myself, then I also know that if he is struggling he doesn't need a sermon, he needs a hug. So I get up off my ass and go hug him. This can be scary sometimes, because we have been taught that if someone is struggling, "that's their stuff" and leave them alone.

When my man is suffering, so am I. One morning we had been arguing and I was sitting at my desk and he was lying on the couch. I thought I would just walk away and leave him to sort it out, but I stopped and asked myself,

> *"If love were standing here right now,*
> *what would it do?"*

My heart knew that he needed some loving more than anything else, so I sucked it up and went and sat with him. It was a wonderful experience. I changed my mind about what to be right about, I decided to be right about how committed I am to our relationship, and went and loved him anyway.

There is already so much pain and suffering in the world, so when we fall in love and make a choice to travel this journey of life with someone, we need to let go of all the pain and suffering out there and just learn to love each other. We need to hold hands and walk together, and as we serve and love each other more, we have more for our children, parents, friends, and everyone else in our world.

And I practise serving and loving in all areas of my life. Practise, practise, practise....

Sometimes I have to practise "What would love do here?" with clenched fists. Several years ago I had ended a relationship and a few months later we found ourselves at the same gathering. There had been a miscommunication about something, and he was very angry and yelling and swearing at me. I reacted by yelling and swearing back. I spent the next hour feeling really horrible about my reaction, and asked myself my favourite question, "What would love do here?" I listened for the answer: I didn't want to spend the rest of my day angry and I didn't want that for him, either, so I approached him to apologize. I asked him if we could get together to talk. He used to take a few days to stew things over, but this day he said, "Great, how about now, let's go outside." I was nervous, but I had resolved that no matter how angry he got I would stay in the place of love. We had a great conversation, we made our peace, had a good laugh, and the next day he died of a massive heart attack.

SOLUTION:

Practise, practise, practise....

ACTION STEP:

Call up three people and ask them, "has anyone told you that they love you today?" If they say, "No," then say, "let me be the first to say I love you." If they respond with yes say, "great, let me tell you also, I love you." It's amazing how many people say "no." I have done this many times, just out of the blue I'll call someone who I haven't seen for a while and they are so touched. When they are touched by that emotion, so am I.

For a more detailed worksheet for this exercise, go to www.OliveJuiceForever.com

- We are here for two reasons: to serve and to love.

- What would love do here?

- Practise serving and loving everyday. Practise, practise, practise.

- When should you start? Now would be good.

PART THREE

Tomorrow

CHAPTER NINE

Games

Have you ever heard of life referred to as a game? If you are playing the game of life, how are you playing? Do you know what game you are playing? Is it hockey or dominoes? Do you play to win? Do you play fair? Are you actually playing or sitting on the sidelines watching?

My biggest game is about love and loving, so when I was sixteen and found out I was having a baby, I was thrilled. What could be greater than carrying another human being and knowing that I would be responsible for guiding them along this journey called life? I was so excited, and my boyfriend was so excited. We planned our wedding and who would be in the wedding party, it was a done deal. Our big game was planned, that was until I got home.

When I put my big game next to my Mum's big game, I found out how different they were: she threw me out of the house. Back then I didn't know love was my big game, so I had no idea that having an abortion was against the very core of my being. At the time, I didn't believe it was my choice to end that baby's chance for a life here on earth. I was young and easily influenced. Three months after the abortion, I was in a hospital bed with a broken back, punctured lung, broken ribs, broken shoulder and many other injuries. Those injuries were nothing next to the pain of my broken heart.

I truly believed that those injuries were nowhere near enough punishment for what I had done. I decided, unconsciously, to spend the rest of my life punishing myself. I was good at it: the accident and later the addictions fuelled my pain.

At twenty two, I gave birth to a beautiful little girl and she became my life. I felt just a little reprieve and thought, if I had one baby and felt a little better, maybe more would relieve me of my guilt. I tried and tried and tried to conceive another child, with all the wrong men for all the wrong reasons. I was never able to carry another baby to full term. Even though I loved my daughter with all my heart and she loved me with all of hers, it wasn't enough. I still couldn't fill that void.

At 27 I was in hospital for another surgery, another one of my near death experiences that I thrived on. Happily I had almost died and sadly I had been pregnant and still no baby. From that experience I ended up in an addiction treatment centre where I started to talk about the abortion and the guilt, the resentment and self loathing. Slowly I started the process of self forgiveness.

A couple of years ago, I was busy renovating a new home. Andrea called me, "what are you doing?" she asked. "I'm painting your room with Michelle." She phoned again and again and again, and every time I was with someone. Finally, she got me alone, at the grocery store. She couldn't keep it in any longer. "Mom, I'm pregnant." I responded with "I'm at the grocery store, you can't tell me this while I'm grocery shopping!" We laughed and I went home to meet her.

It was a long ten minute drive home, and I really didn't know what to do or say. What I did know was that the decision was hers and that whatever she chose to do I would support her one hundred percent. I love my daughter as I know my mother loves me. I also knew that breaking the cycle of pain gave all three of us a gift: the gift of putting the past in the past, and the gift of a beautiful child, Faith Annie.

We all need big games to play in life. If I don't have a big game then I won't play big. In fact, I may not even play at all but just tend to move along life doing what I think I need to be doing, or what other people tell me to do, and then die.

I may have a game that isn't shared with my partner and we end up resenting each other's games, resentful of the passion, time and attention they are putting into their game of life, especially if I don't have one. I am not saying that it doesn't work to have your own passions, it absolutely does. What I am saying is that to have a common game is exciting and keeps you playing together.

The more games you have in common the greater the probability of the relationship lasting. With common games there's lots to talk about, new experiences to share and things and places to explore.

A big game is bigger than all the little things that can take you out, the fighting over money, the kids, the in-laws, and the chores. A big game keeps you focused on what really matters in your own lives. A big game keeps life exciting and fun.

We have several common big games, and our biggest is our company, Olive Juice Forever. We are extremely dedicated to our game. It's fun, challenging and intimate, and satisfies all of our driving needs. Talk about a win/win.

Being a couple of love junkies, we knew that intimacy was a big driving need for both of us, so it seemed fitting that we start a business that is all about love. I was already teaching some of the principles that are in this book, and most of the stories are our own. We both knew we wanted to contribute to making the world a better place. We do that by sharing our message: love *is* the answer.

We started at the beach with a notebook and a pen and a bunch of ideas. What do we want to create? Why? Who is our audience? Why? We wrote down a couple of pages of what we wanted to create. Once we had written down our goals and strategies, we laid back, closed our eyes and talked ourselves through a visualization, setting our intentions. Then we went home and carried on with our everyday life.

We didn't immediately start breaking the goals into monthly and weekly steps, but we knew what we were going to create. We would talk about it often, clarifying and refining our goals and strategies. Eleven months later, most of those goals were achieved, and the rest were well under way. Our first goal was to write this book that you are now reading.

In playing the game of life, most people choose their partner, have a couple of children, buy a home and have their careers, but then what? They become comfortable and complacent in their lives and I have often heard people ask "is this all there is?" What do you do once you have the house, career, kids? Keep cutting the grass and saving for the next vacation?

When I first start playing a game I am usually full of passion and excitement, the challenge is intense and I am "in." When I have been playing the same game for a while the excitement wears off and I feel the need to be challenged elsewhere. My passion and participation dwindle, unless I have created ways to stay excited and challenged and committed to the game.

SOLUTION:

How many of us actually know what our big games are? Very few.

I want to take you through a simple visualization process. Imagine your life is a big glass jar. Fill it with rocks from the pile next to it, fill it right up to the top. Is the jar full? No. From the bucket beside the jar, scoop out some gravel, and pour it in, let it trickle down and fill the spaces between the rocks. Is the jar full yet? No. Scoop up sand from beneath your feet. And let it trickle down into the spaces between the rocks and gravel.

Is the jar full? No. Pick up the jug, and pour water into your jar, until it is full, right up to the top.

The sand and water are all the basic things from the bottom of Maslow's pyramid of needs: food, sleep, safety and security. The gravel is the bigger needs like community, status, dignity, confidence and achievement. The rocks are our big games, the goals and dreams that really matter to us, that so often get left on a shelf somewhere.

So many people fill their lives, their jar, with sand and water, maybe a bit of gravel, that there's no room for their big rocks. If you haven't done it already, now is the time to start to formulate your big games. These could be around health, or family, or community. It could be a business venture or a spiritual quest. You could have several big games or rocks, of all different sizes, or only one or two big rocks that combine several ideas.

One of our big games is family, and within that game a top goal is creating a safe place for our family to live. We are committed to having a home that is big enough and comfortable enough for any of our family to feel welcome with us. Another goal in this game is bi-weekly family dinner nights, it's chaos for a few hours, and we love it. A family dream is to travel to the North Pole at Christmas time.

If one of your big games as a couple is to create a safe and loving home for your children and extended family, then you may want to look at reading some parenting books together or setting up family time. You might take some parenting courses or find something that you all like to do as a family and make time for that to happen.

Remember that you are committed to this together. When you are playing a big game of life, on the same team, when challenges come up you'll be able to deal with them and move along, because you have a much bigger game to play than who didn't put down the toilet seat or empty the dishwasher.

Action Step:

The more we engage in playing this common game together, the higher the probability of our relationship lasting. Our common games keep me searching for evidence of all the good in the world, and staying on track with my goals and dreams.

What are your big games? What dreams have been left on a shelf somewhere? Go back to when you were a kid and start there. What did you want to be when you grew up? Are you that? Is it still a dream? What are your big dreams now?

What are your common games and goals as a couple? I always had a dream to write a book and Shawn always wanted to start a company. We put the two together, and Olive Juice Forever was born.

If figuring out your big games seems a bit overwhelming, start with a smaller goal that will lead you to your big game. Once you've picked a dream or goal, WRITE IT DOWN! Now develop three strategies you can take to achieve this goal, and write them down.

Perhaps you always wanted to be an actor, so find an acting course in your community. If you've always wanted to own a restaurant, go to cooking school or take a restaurant management course. Maybe you want to own your own home or business, invest in real estate, travel to exotic places, spend a year volunteering overseas, and so on.

1. Identify a big goal or dream.
2. WRITE IT DOWN.
3. Create three strategies to achieve it.

If, for example, you want to go to college, it will look like this:

Goal: get my college degree in _____.
1. Find a school with this program.
2. Find out entrance requirements and costs.
3. Get registration forms and decide when to start. Put a date on it.

For a more detailed worksheet for this exercise, go to www.OliveJuiceForever.com

- What does your current game of life look like?

- As a couple, the more games you have in common, the greater the probability of your relationship lasting.

- What are your goals and dreams? Are they written down?

CHAPTER TEN

Dreams

From the time I was six, I knew I wanted to write a book. It seemed like a pipe dream, such a big dream that I never wrote it down or ever imagined it could come true. That was my problem: I never, ever imagined that it could come true.

Becoming an addict also wasn't on my goal list. When I found myself, at 27 years old, in a treatment center being encouraged to practise affirmations, I thought to myself, "I'm good at affirmations, I just haven't chosen positive ones." I was taught there that we become what we think about most of the time so I thought I would give them a shot. They gave us some examples to try.

I love and accept myself unconditionally.

Well, that was pretty funny, but I tried it. I would say it, "I love and accept myself unconditionally," and then my next thought would be "you must be joking, you *@#% loser," followed by, "no, no, no, I love and accept myself unconditionally." That one didn't work because I didn't believe it. However, I did discover that I can only have one thought at a time and that while I am thinking the positive thought (whether I believed it or not), I wasn't thinking a negative one.

I started reading different books and figured out that I could poison my mind or feed it some loving thoughts. I read about other people who had been down and out and how they changed their minds and changed their lives.

I become what I think about, and affirmations helped me to stay away from the negative thoughts and feelings I was having about myself most of the time. I chose easy ones like:

I always act, think and speak
in a positive manner.

I am happy.

I spent many nights falling asleep reciting the serenity prayer. So simple:

God, grant me the serenity
to accept the things I cannot change,
the courage to change the things I can,
and the wisdom to know the difference.

I noticed that I would wake up feeling happier and more relaxed and my days got better. Eventually I began to make different choices in my life and I became a lot happier as a result.

This stuff was very foreign to me when I went to treatment and started hearing about positive thinking and living a life of happiness and joy. Freedom was a word that was used a lot and I loved that word. I wanted to be free from the ties that bind. Free from addiction and self loathing. This stuff really wasn't attractive, and energetically it sucked the life out of me and out of the people around me. Negative energy is powerful and dark and draining. Funny how when I am feeling crappy I spend a lot of time on the couch or somewhere feeling sorry for myself and it takes all the energy I have to drag my sorry ass around. On the other hand when I am feeling good about myself I can accomplish anything and usually do. They (whoever they are) say that we are all made up of energy and I have the power to decide who and what I want to become.

It's hard to visualize something great when I am still in hate with myself. Until I believed that I deserved all my dreams I wasn't having any of them. I needed to clear my mind of all the old cobwebs first. I had to learn to believe that I deserved good things in life.

It really doesn't take much to change our lives. If I decided today that I was going to change from earning $50,000 a year to 100K, it would be somewhat scary and hard to fathom those changes right away, and then there is the question of how would I achieve that kind of increase in income? What I have come to understand is that we have a comfort zone that we create for ourselves and we create it early in life. We decide at some point what we are worth in love, money, happiness and everything, then we go and create that for ourselves. We get comfortable, and if we never become aware of wanting more out of life, we will never change. If I want to go from 50K to 100K, how do I do it if my comfort zone says I am worth between 40K and 60K per year?

I take it one step at a time and find or attract ways to increase my net worth. I may change jobs with an increase in pay or I may take on a commission-based job and start to increase my income that way. If I get too much too soon my level of comfort will be way off my scale and my brilliant mind will find a way to disregard my new found wealth. We have all heard stories about someone who was down and out and won the lottery and then two years later they are broke again. One of those rags to riches stories, until the story goes from riches back to rags again. Statistics show that most who win the lottery will be broke again within a few years.

Personally my story around money used to be that if I had any money in the bank it was too much and I would find lots of ways to spend it. I always had new clothes and lots of stuff, and I always needed something new. When I started taking the Excellence Series I had no money, I was living in a little two-bedroom condo with my daughter and driving an older car, but we were doing all right.

We were always doing just all right, but if something happened that I needed money right away, there was no savings or other resources to find the money. The bank certainly wouldn't be doling out money to me to finance some great idea or a book. When I changed my mind about my self worth and net worth, all of a sudden going shopping for me became a chore.

I changed my mind about my self worth, and gradually my life changed. There was a time if I had $1,000 in the bank I would have to spend it, and today if I only have $1,000 in my checking account, I am very uncomfortable. I am only using money as an example because it is measurable. I cannot begin to tell you how much my comfort level of love and trust has increased.

Once I knew that what I really want in life exists above my current level of comfort, I got to work remembering, imagining and visualizing my heart's desires.

So far I had not been able to maintain a long term relationship, but I knew I really wanted a long term, intimate relationship with a man who shares my values and has similar dreams. A few years ago I got together with a group of people and we started really working on our long term visions. We made a list of 9 areas in our lives to focus on and wrote about each of them. Part of mine was to attract a husband and what I wrote was:

...and that he has to be funny, funny, funny.

If you had asked me at any time who do I think is the funniest person I know I would have said Shawn Jensen, although he certainly didn't come to mind when I wrote that vision. A year later he read the vision I had written and it was so close to reality that he thought I had just written it.

I took that outline of what my life would look like and read it out loud to the group I was working with and I did something different, I believed it, and within no time it began to manifest. The result: I am married to the greatest, funniest guy alive, we live in a beautiful home surrounded by love and we have finished our first book. We are healthy, happy and living our big game.

SOLUTION:

Visualizing doesn't have to be done from the top of a mountain for three hours a day. I practise by closing my eyes as I am waiting for my vehicle to warm up and see my vision then. I take a few moments and see my picture, I can feel the feeling when I am in it and I see it as if I have already achieved it.

We currently have a picture of our long term vision framed and hanging on our wall and we have a collage of things and events we are creating together hanging on our bedroom wall. Seeing those pictures on a daily basis, I continue to feed my mind with images of what I want. I stand in front of our collage and just relax and breathe. I see, in my mind's eye, myself in that picture and then I can slow down. Sometimes I become over-whelmed, and just looking at that collection of maga-zine cut-outs of what I want to achieve brings me back to the here and now, and I am reminded that my pent up frustration is not assisting me in moving closer to my dreams.

Okay, we've reached the point in the book where some of you guys are thinking, "Would somebody stop the madness?"

If you had asked me a year ago about visualizing, I'd be visualizing Lorraine, and that's about it. And if you had asked me 5 years ago about this visualization stuff, I would have said, "stay away from me you freak," or, "my mind doesn't have an eye," or more to the point, "get off my property."

But I've grown since those days, and now when we go through our struggles, I think about that long term vision picture we have created together, and it brings me back. Two steps forward, one back. As long as we're moving closer to our goals, it's okay if we deviate from our direction and then course correct. But if we don't know where we're going, we'll never, ever get there.

Our long term vision helps to bring me back to what's most important to us: each other and our family.

I don't know, I'm just a guy.

Shawn

I know some of this sounds like a lot of work and a bit airy fairy, but you know what? When I hear the Tiger Woods and Wayne Gretzky's of the world talk about setting their goals and clearly seeing them and then achieving them, I figure what have I got to lose?

ACTION STEP:

In my mind, affirmations and visualizations are positive thoughts that replace negative ones. I use them to declare what I want, as if I already have it. And it takes practise.

Take your goal from Chapter 9, close your eyes and see yourself as if you have already achieved it. If going to college is your goal, visualize walking across the stage to receive your degree. Or imagine holding the first copy of your first book. Whatever your goal is, create a powerful and positive vision of being in the process of achieving it. Go to sleep, wake up, live 24/7 with your vision clear in your mind.

If you can dream it, you can do it.
Walt Disney

For a more detailed worksheet for this exercise, go to www.OliveJuiceForever.com

◉ Change your mind and change your life.

◉ Where is your comfort level set?

◉ Can you close your eyes and see your goal at completion? Can you touch, taste, see and feel it?

OLIVE JUICE FOREVER

CHAPTER ELEVEN

Support

When I quit drinking I weighed 108 lbs. At my one year cake, I was up to 150 lbs. I don't know if anyone else had noticed an extra 42lbs on my 5'3" frame, but I certainly wasn't going to bring it up. It killed me every time I stopped on the way home to buy something to stuff those feelings. How could food have so much power over me? At the time I could understand the alcohol, but a cookie running my life! I had overcome so much in my 28 years and now to give it all up to food seemed insane. I often wondered if I would ever be happy.

I was so ashamed, I couldn't possibly talk about it and I decided to go to an OA meeting (Overeaters Anonymous). There were meetings all over the place, but the one I chose to attend was in another town, across a bridge in a place where I knew no one. I went there, petrified. What if someone saw me? What if nothing changed? Most of the attendees looked at me like I had three heads, as my weight really wasn't an issue to them, but to me it was the end of the world. I was horrified when I found out that the meeting was in the library, in a room surrounded by windows. Then, in the middle of the meeting, someone knocked on the window. I turned and almost died when I saw a guy from work standing there, genuinely happy to see me and waving hello. Well, I was out of there and never going back.

I had another brain wave: I would go and work for a weight loss center, that way I could learn all the tricks of the trade, lose all my weight and nobody would be the wiser. So I did, I went and took all the training and was so excited about the opportunity to be a weight loss counselor, thinking I would do nothing but lose weight as I would be inspired by all the people I was helping. Well, the company had other ideas and they hired me as a manager and I never got to assist clients and my job was stressful and my commute was long, long enough to stop a couple of times on the way home to buy more food to numb my pain.

The warrior woman in me was so invested in protecting my already battered self image, that I couldn't possibly ask for any more help. It had taken everything I had to ask to go into treatment, and here I was, a year later, shoving cookies into my mouth. I had overcome my drinking and drugging, but I was in the same place again with a different poison. How dare I ask for more help? Not asking was killing me.

When I look back on the major challenges I have faced in my life, it was only at those times when I finally dropped my shield and started talking honestly about my feelings and fears that I was able to get the support I craved. With support, I was able to walk again, quit drinking, keep my child, get through the death of a loved one, and make a whole bunch of positive changes in my life. With all the evidence throughout my life proving that support is a good thing, why did I always felt so weak when reaching out for help?

One of the things I do in my career is coach people and I am good at it. I get to support people as they learn to stretch and reach for their goals and dreams. I'm really good at giving support, but I'm not so good at asking for it. Sometimes it just shows up.

A few months after Shawn and I got married, I was having a chat with my daughter, Andrea, about my relationship with Shawn. She looked me square in the eye and she said, "Mum, I know what you have been through and I have watched you change from a woman finding love in so many negative ways, to being a true example of love in action. I am really proud of you AND if you ever start looking for any back doors in this relationship, I will hunt you down, lock you in your room, and keep you there until you come to your senses." Now that's support.

A good friend of mine kept telling me about the coach she had hired and then she would tell me about the advances she was making in her business. I was jealous and wanted to create those kind of results for myself but was still not willing to ask...oh, so that's the stopping place...asking for support. Why would I ask for help when I teach this stuff? I should know better. Well, knowing and doing are clearly two different things.

Why wouldn't I hire a coach, is it pride? What will people say? Well, I can tell you what people were saying: nothing. There was nothing to say because I wasn't doing anything. I finally got it. No matter who we are or where we are in life, support is essential to help us reach our goals.

SOLUTION:

So I changed my mind, and we hired a business coach to help us sort out our business plan. Once we developed a business plan we put it all into action. There were times when I thought I couldn't do it, that writing a book was too big, I didn't have anything to say, I don't have a degree, it was going to take up too much time, and the list goes on. Then I would reach out to the people who had agreed to be our support, and found myself refocusing and getting back on track. We asked a group of people to read our book and offer us feedback and that was great support. We purchased books on how to write books and the work seemed like it would never end. I hired someone to edit and someone else to re-edit and we had the book cover designed and it still seemed like the work would never end. It did. This book is now complete, we have our company set up and our marketing plan is under way. We are thrilled with our results.

We have a support team and it works.

ACTION STEP:

Make a list of the people you know who could support you in moving closer to your dreams, to help you achieve the goal you wrote down in the previous chapter's action step.

If you can't think of anyone in your immediate circle, look beyond who you know. There are so many resources out there, diet centers, anonymous programs, baby groups, counselors, pastors, tutors, cooking schools, writing groups, personal trainers, personal coaches…why do we think we have to do it alone?

Find somebody who can help you to achieve your goal, someone who has skill or knowledge in that area. Ask them to be on your team.

For a more detailed worksheet for this exercise, go to www.OliveJuiceForever.com

- Support is essential to help us reach our goals.
- Can you ask for support when you need it?
- Who is on your support team?

CHAPTER TWELVE

Celebration

Do we celebrate enough? Why do people get honoured and celebrated when they die? I would rather have the party while I am still alive so I can pick out my own clothes. The only thing is I don't know when I am going to die, so I had best remember to always wear the good stuff and celebrate the successes every day.

Most of us celebrate national holidays, anniversaries, and birthdays once a year. When we get married there's a big ceremony and celebration and then nothing for 365 days. That's a long time to wait and there are many events that happen in that year that probably deserve a lot of celebrating, like the hurdles you overcome as you start to learn how to live together. Each celebration offers more opportunity to honour the work you are doing and is an opportunity to create more evidence of all the love and happiness that surrounds you both.

We pretend that we are Johnny Cash and June Carter Cash, and to take a line from our favourite Johnny and June song, "Jackson," when we got married, "we got married in a fever." We were dressed like them, Shawn all in black with cufflinks that said 'Johnny' and me in a great vintage dress, and we had fun. We didn't tell anyone and invited our families over, for what we told them was a family picture, and surprised them all. We got married kneeling on our round bed. Then we went and celebrated with 150 people at an event I was hosting for a program that Shawn was graduating from. Our wedding was great and different and uniquely ours. We loved the intimacy of planning it together and the intensity of keeping the secret. We also received lots of attention that evening.

One of the events that inspired this book was when people caught wind of our Johnny and June game and wanted to know how to create more fun in their own lives. We have fun because we have committed to having fun. And it is hard work, any relationship is hard work. I believe that when you commit to the journey and start doing the work necessary to break through the fear, give up the power struggles and stay above the line, forgive yourself and others, and get yourself out of image, then things will start to change for you. Once you start figuring out what drives you and commit to getting those needs met constructively, trust love over fear, ask yourself what would love do here, create a big game for yourself, set your goals, and find the support you need, there'll be no turning back.

Celebrate at any time! The more fun we create for ourselves, the harder we are willing to work. Shawn and I work hard in our relationship and we celebrate a lot along the way. When we created our big game, we knew that it would be a lot of work and we were both willing to take it on. We also knew about ourselves and each other that attention was another driving need we both shared and it would be good to include ways to get the attention and intimacy met in really positive ways. So we sat down one day and made a list of how we would celebrate our relationship and honour all the work we have committed to doing together.

One strategy is to take one day a month and make it our free day; we wake up in the morning and do whatever we want. Sometimes we go for a walk or a run, we have a favourite restaurant we frequent for breakfast, we stay in bed if we want to, or we go on a day trip. We book this day in our calendars early every month and that's it: no phones, email or anything that will distract us from "our" day.

Our other favourite strategy is every other month we take turns creating a romantic date for each other. We never know when it's coming during the month and we don't know what it will be. We have set up some ground rules and promise to always keep it safe. We both have driving needs for intimacy and intensity so it works for both of us to keep the excitement alive.

We love the loving and always look forward to the surprise. It's also a great way to grow deeper in our relationship as we are continually creating more intimacy, trust and faith in each other. Our monthly date is just one of the rewards we have created for all the hard work we have committed to in our relationship.

Not all couples are going to feel comfortable engaging in some of the escapades we get up to but that is where your sense of adventure comes into play. If you are interested in some ideas, we publish our monthly "Create-a-Date" on our website, www.OliveJuiceForever.com

Your monthly date can be as simple as inviting your loved one to join you for a walk along the beach or as creative as planning a night on the town. It could be taking time to write and mail a love letter or it could be a bit more daring, like calling from a pay phone and having phone sex with each other.

> I know how I'd like to celebrate, but I'll need a quarter....
> Just a guy.
> **Shawn**

We write love notes all the time, and when we feel inspired one of us will write in our notes-to-each-other journal and leave the book out for the other to see.

Being a couple of love junkies we love to love and we love to have fun, so celebrating is something we really like to do. It was really important for us to get married, as we both believe that our commitment to the game is as big as the game itself.

And we are committed to our game. In our Olive Juice game, we get to participate in the big game of life. We both acknowledge that we have brought baggage packed with fear, resentment and mistrust. We also know that under and mixed in with all that muck is a whole pile of love, gratitude and acceptance. We are willing to put down our masks and ask ourselves "what would love do here," before we ask the other "what are you afraid of right now?" We know we are getting our driving needs met and our goals reflect the direction we are choosing to take in life. Creating this book was a big leap of faith. Everyday we celebrate our lives together.

We have felt our luggage become lighter and lighter as we move forward together and as individuals, forging through some of the muck we have dragged along with us. I believe that as long as I am still breathing, I will continue to learn and for that I will always be truly grateful.

You can choose to commit to your life at any time and you can find times to celebrate throughout the journey. Our life is the journey and I want to celebrate every day, however big or small. I want to stay grateful and humble and I never want to forget who I am and why I am here. I keep on building my pile of good evidence, evidence of how much I love and am loved, evidence of how much love there really is in the world, and what a wonderful life I really have.

And then I say, "thank you."

OLIVE JUICE FOREVER

- to purchase more books and other products
- to subscribe to our monthly newsletter
- to subscribe to our love-spirational quotes
- to find out about our speaking engagements
- check in to see what other couples are asking Lorraine and Shawn
- to get some ideas about the monthly Create-a-Date

go to our website: www.OliveJuiceForever.com

To contact us: info@OliveJuiceForever.com

1.877.OliveJF
(1.877.654-8353)

About the Authors

Lorraine Jensen was born in London, England and moved to Canada when she was twelve. Lorraine is a highly energetic facilitator, trainer and personal coach who has worked with people in many capacities over the span of her diverse career. She has worked in sales and training, and has provided counseling and coordinated centres that support people struggling with drug, alcohol and food addictions. Lorraine's personal life experiences and challenges, coupled with her sense of humour, genuine enthusiasm and love for life, provide hope and inspiration to others.

Shawn Jensen was born and raised in Canada, and spent the first five years of his working life in the Canadian navy. He went on to become a leader in the field of Human Resources, where he has mastered the skill of negotiation and conflict resolution. Shawn has achieved personal and professional success in spite of his intense sense of humour and kind, gentle nature.

Shawn and Lorraine live in Nanaimo, B.C., in a large home they share with Andrea, Niall, Erin and Faith.